2015© Copyright by B. A. Anderson
Roxie The SuperCat Saves Christmas

All rights reserved. No part of this book may be reproduced or transmitted in any form or by any means electronically or mechanical, including photocopying, recording, without the written permission of the author. Text, illustrations, logos and cover design by DM BOOKPRO.

Website: RoxieTheSuperCat.com
Publishing Services: DMBookPro.com

Paperback ISBN:978-0692581339

Printed in the USA
Visit our website RoxieTheSuperCat.com for FREE gifts and Roxie SuperCat Items.

DEDICATION
We dedicate this book to Sandy Oglesby, who encouraged and inspired, us with her gifts in so many ways and who saved our Christmas. Sandy has a gift with words and is an outstanding storyteller and you can find her at:

StorytellerSandy.com

IT WAS THE NIGHT BEFORE CHRISTMAS WHEN ALL THROUGH THE SHELTER,

NOT A CREATURE WAS STIRRING NOT EVEN THE ONLY DOG IN THIS SHELTER.

The stockings were hung on the mantel with great care,

Hopeful that donations would fill cupboards now bare;

THE KITTENS WERE PURRING, SNUGGLED ALL WARM IN THEIR BEDS,

WHILE VISIONS OF CATNIP AND TREATS DANCED IN THEIR HEADS;

THIS CHRISTMAS WAS DREADFUL - NO FUNDS FOR CAT TOYS OR CAT TREATS,

WE TRIED TO KEEP ENOUGH CAT LITTER AND THE HOUSE FULL OF GOOD EATS;

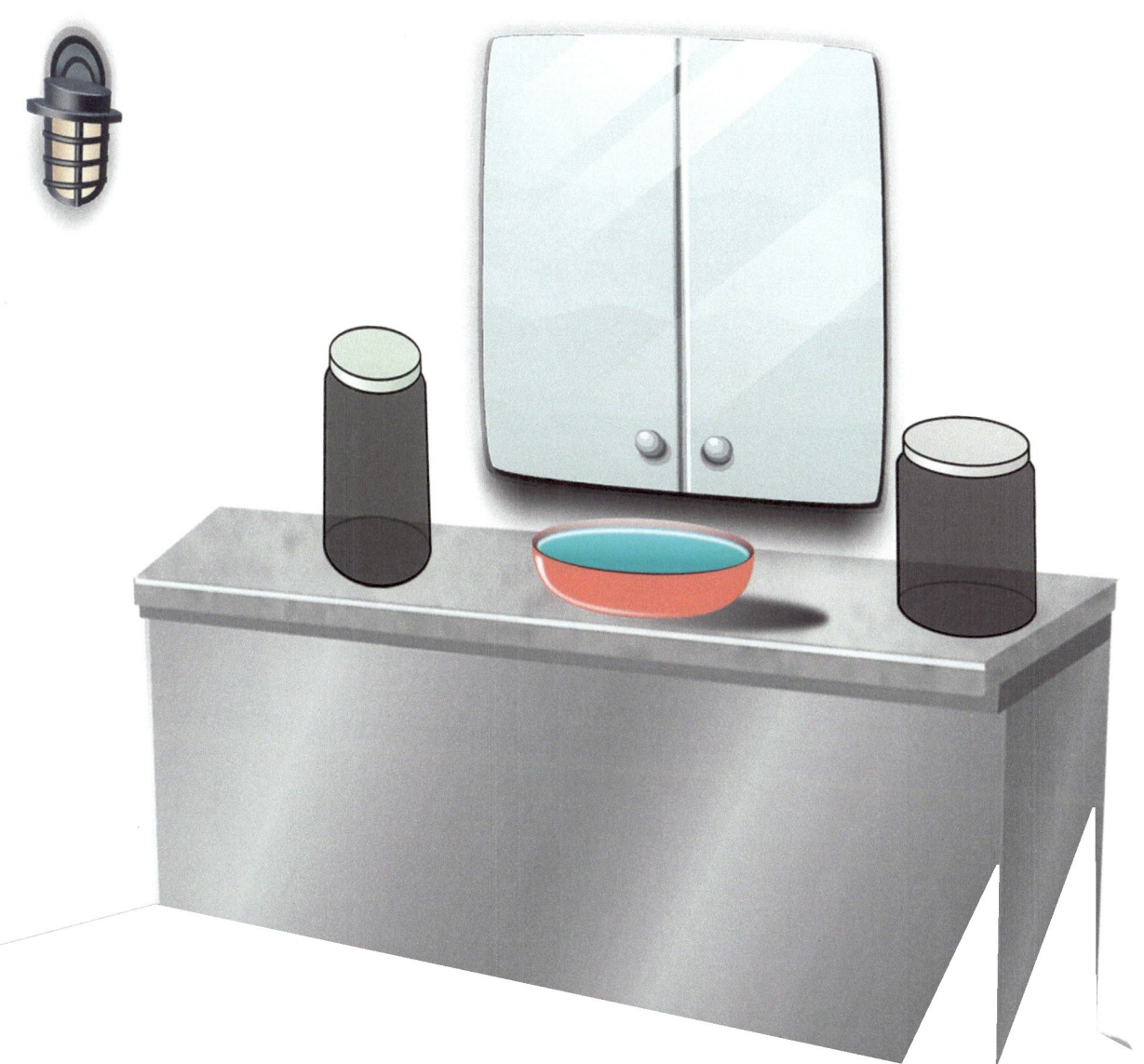

THE SHELTER MISTRESS WAS NAPPING ALL CURLED UP IN HER CHAIR,

WHILE SHE WORRIED ABOUT OVER-CROWDING, AND GENERAL CAT CARE;

OUT ON THE ROOFTOP, BANG, BOOM! WHAT CLATTER!

SHE SPRANG TO HER FEET TO SEE WHAT WAS THE MATTER;

OUT THROUGH THE DOOR SHE FLEW LIKE A FLASH,

SHE KNOCKED THE WATER BOWL AND MADE A BIG SPLASH.

THE MOON SHOWN BRIGHTLY ON THE NEW FALLEN SNOW,

GIVING A BRIGHT LUSTER TO ALL OBJECTS BELOW.

WELL WHAT TO HER WONDERING EYES SHOULD APPEAR?

BUT A FLYING CAT, A SLEIGH AND SOME REINDEER;

SHE SAID VERY QUIETLY, "PLEASE COME DOWN TO THE GROUND,"

"YOU WILL WAKE THE KITTENS AND THEY WILL RUN AROUND,"

THAT CAT FLEW AROUND AND CAME DOWN TO THE GROUND,

THE SLEIGH AND REINDEER FOLLOWED WITHOUT A SOUND;

THE CAT WHISTLED AND CALLED THE REINDEER BY NAME,

WHILE SHE SMILED, SO GLAD THAT THEY CAME;

IT WAS ROXIE THE SUPERCAT WITH A HUGE SLEIGH FULL OF GOODIES,

DONATIONS OF CAT TREATS, CAT TOYS, LITTER AND YUMMY FOODIES;

ROXIE THE SUPERCAT HAD A LONG CAPE OF RED,

WEARING A WHITE FUR LINED CAP ON HER HEAD;

ROXIE HAD DARK FUR FROM HER HEAD TO HER FEET,

SHE WORE A RED JACKET AND LOOKED REALLY SWEET;

SHE GRABBED THE RED BAG STUFFED FULL WITH THOSE TREATS,

THE MISTRESS WONDERED: WILL THERE BE ANY GRAVY WITH MEATS;

GREAT BUNDLES OF STUFF WAS FLUNG ON HER BACK,

HOW COULD SHE CARRY SUCH A STUFFED PACK?;

COULD ROXIE THE SUPERCAT SAVE THE SHELTER ON THIS CHRISTMAS DAY?

SHE MEOWED AND SHE NODDED AND THE MISTRESS GOT OUT OF THE WAY;

SHE CAME RIGHT INSIDE AND WENT STRAIGHT TO HER WORK,

FILLED UP THE STOCKINGS AND THEN TURNED WITH A JERK;

ROXIE PUT EVEN MORE WONDERFUL GIFTS UNDER THE TREE,

THE MISTRESS CRIED OUT, SHE WAS SO GRATEFUL YOU SEE;

THERE WERE BAGS OF DRY CAT FOOD AND CAT LITTER,

THE MISTRESS GOT SO EXCITED SHE BEGAN TO JITTER;

ROXIE DID BRING CANNED GRAVY WITH MEATS,

AND SO MANY BAGS OF YUMMY CAT TREATS;

ROXIE SMILED AT A PURRING TABBY CAT,

THEN REACHED TO ADJUST HER FUR HAT;

SHE LOOKED AROUND AT ALL THE KITTENS,

WHILE HOLDING HER RED FURRY MITTENS;

THEN SHE SWALLOWED A GREEN TUNA TREAT,

THE MISTRESS WONDERED IF THEY WERE SOUR OR SWEET?;

ROXIE GAZED AROUND AT THE STOCKINGS AND TREE,

SHE SMILED AND PUT HER CAT ARMS AROUND ME;

IT WAS ROXIE WHO SAVED THIS CHRISTMAS DAY,

SHE SAVED CHRISTMAS IN HER OWN SPECIAL WAY;

ROXIE FLEW TO THE SLEIGH, GAVE A NOD TO HER TEAM,

THEY FLEW TO THE NEXT SHELTER IN SUCH A FAST STREAM;

I HEARD HER EXCLAIM, AS THEY FLEW OUT OF SIGHT,

"MERRY CHRISTMAS TO ALL, AND TO ALL A GOOD NIGHT!"

CAT SHELTERS HAVE MANY KITTENS TO FEED,

LITTER AND CAT FOOD ARE TWO BASIC NEEDS;

WHEN YOU DECIDE TO ADOPT A CAT OR A KITTEN,

GO TO A SHELTER, YOU WILL SURELY BE SMITTEN!

ROXIE THE SUPERCAT WORKED HARD TO SAVE CHRISTMAS THIS YEAR.

WHEN YOU VISIT A SHELTER THE REASON WILL BE CLEAR.

PERHAPS IN THE FUTURE YOU CAN HELP MY DEAR!

Thank you for getting a copy of this book. We hope you enjoyed reading about how Roxie The SuperCat saved The Night Before Christmas.

Please visit our website RoxieTheSuperCat.com for Supercat products, coloring books and games. We will have giveaways, prizes and keep you updated with more books in Roxie The SuperCat Series!

If you had a nice reading experience, it would really help us and leave a review on Amazon. Your review might just encourage someone else to get this book for their loved ones.

Thank You,

Barb Anderson owned by Roxie The SuperCat

Every year in the U.S., more than 6 million lost, abandoned, or unwanted dogs and cats enter animal shelters.

Some of these dogs and cats are lucky enough to be adopted into loving, responsible, and permanent homes. But there are far more animals in need of a caring family than there are kind people willing to provide them with a good, permanent home.

People still buy animals from breeders or pet stores (thereby supporting the puppy mills that supply them) instead of adopting homeless animals. And people acquire companion animals without considering the lifetime commitment that caring for them requires. Eventually, people turn their backs on their loyal companions when they become "inconvenient" or "too much work."

You can help by telling your friends to adopt a pet from the shelter. They can also donate to animal shelters to help support the cause and provide food and vet care. Tell everyone you know to get their animal spayed or neutered, so we can help eliminate homeless animals.

Visit RoxieTheSuperCat to learn how Roxie was adopted from a cat shelter. Learn how she received her super powers and what she does for fun.

www.ingramcontent.com/pod-product-compliance
Lightning Source LLC
LaVergne TN
LVHW072113070426
835510LV00002B/35